Rabbit Chinese Horoscope 2024

By
IChingHun FengShuisu

Table of Contents

Introduce

The character of people born in the year of the RABBIT

People born in the Rabbit year are gentle and caring. You are also a good friend and condescending person, in addition to having a kind, sweet, and affectionate nature. I dislike making others unhappy. Rabbits appreciate beauty, are artistic, and have refined taste. Despite being loved by friends and family, Rabbits remain pessimistic, fearful, conservative, and easily insecure. making it someone who dislikes change.

People born this year are reserved, making it difficult to awaken the rabbit's mood. In any case, he dislikes arguing and prefers a quiet life. Frequently timid or skeptical That is, rabbits frequently have to weigh the pros and cons before deciding what to do.

Strength:
Rabbit people are well-mannered people who are always loved by everyone.

Weaknesses:
Likes to be alone dislikes loud noises, is easily startled, and can be overly timid at times.

Love:
People born in this year are sensitive, gentle, fanciful, and less firm in their love. If you want to love someone born in the year of the Rabbit, you must be willing to endure some pain. Don't expect the bunnies to last. He or she has a weak heart. If someone comes to do good deeds with them, they are enthralled and can't take their eyes off them. People born this year are notoriously envious. Because if you love someone, you usually won't let anyone else take it away from you. People born in this year prefer to always create an atmosphere of new love. couples born this year There is no boredom or emotionlessness. It also has a strong love mood.

Suitable Career:
People born in the Year of the Rabbit belong to the Wood element. Known occupations are thus primarily related to wood, such as tree

planting, landscaping, furniture making, wood trading, or work related to business trips related to telecommunications or work that requires extensive contact and negotiation with people, such as guides. Create a tour company, hire a DJ, and work in public relations. Department coordination, sales, creative, selling mobile phones or satellite dishes, and so on, including export business and dealing with foreigners. All of these occupations are appropriate for the Year of the Rabbit.

Year of the RABBIT (Earth) | (1939) & (1999)
"The RABBIT in the Wild" is a person born in the year of the RABBIT at the age of 85 years (1939) and 25 years (1999)

Overview
The planet that orbits into your destined abode this year is the "Ngek Tung Star" for the senior destined person of the Year of the Rabbit, this age cycle. This year, fortunate stars are supporting and shining brilliantly, making the

path of work and finances profitable and worry-free. Because you are an aged person, you should prioritize your own health care. Emphasis on eating hygiene - locate a caregiver to accompany you while traveling or conducting outdoor activities. Be aware that falling might result in injury and hazard. You should learn to let go of things. Avoid being overly engaged in your children's lives. You simply stand back and observe from a safe distance.

Because the planet that orbits into your horoscope this year is "Jimui," for young individuals in the Year of the Rabbit around this age, this year is regarded another lucky moment in which you will experience positive changes. May you have the guts to move forward, to grow and to adapt in order to stay up with the times. Make the most of technological tools and equipment. Because of job and business, you will discover the strength of assistance this year. There will be grownups to support you no matter what you believe, read, or do. It is also a good moment to take action and follow your ambitions. For those of you who desire to start your own company. This year will be seen as an excellent time to open a modest store, but only if there are a lot of clients. More individuals will be aware, and the firm will steadily expand to attain the aim. Despite the fact that the cash may be insufficient. This year, though, you will have adult assistance. It provides the dream a chance to come true. The rationale for starting this this year is because the zodiac signs have the ability to help one another. Starting at the right moment implies less risk and error. As a result, in order to achieve your objectives flawlessly, you must be hardworking and patient.

Career and Business

This year will be beneficial for those that work for their destinies in both life cycles. In many enterprises, I discovered the path to success. Most of the time, everything goes swimmingly. As a result, this is the year to resolve to be more vigilant. Dare to make your aspirations a reality. Dare to enter the stock market or invest in something you are passionate about if a good chance arises. You must understand how to seize it. The 2nd Chinese month (5 Mar. - 3 Apr.), the 6th Chinese month (6 Jul. - 6 Aug.), the 9th Chinese month (8 Oct. - 6 Nov.), and the 10th Chinese month (7 Nov. - 5 Dec.) are the months that support and promote you in your endeavor to move to the next level. However, you should use caution in the next months when working, especially business. There will be commercial impediments and issues, including the 3rd Chinese month (4 April - 4 May), the 5th Chinese month (5 Jun. - 5 Jul.), and the 8th Chinese month (7 Sep. - 7 Oct.). and the 11th Chinese month (6 Dec. '24 - 4 Jan '25).

Be wary of subordinates or persons close to you who cause troubles and anguish. To heighten prudence, both in forming various legal contracts. Be wary of being duped by fraudsters or having your money stolen by insiders.

Financial
Financial fortune: The stars are aligned in favor of wealth this year. Money is flowing in either directly from salaries or indirectly from

sales of goods or services. Money from extra employment, commissions, bonuses, and other sources of income, as well as money from windfalls, all pass through your hands. Especially during the months when finances are flowing freely, such as the 2nd Chinese month (5 Mar. - 3 Apr.), the 6th Chinese month (6 Jul. - 6 Aug.), the 9th Chinese month (8 Oct. - 6 Nov.), and the 10th Chinese month (7 Nov. - 5 Dec.), if you are extremely vigilant. If you dare to invest during the months that support you, you will get more wealth. The anticipated dividends will undoubtedly be received at the end of the fiscal year. However, you should exercise caution during the month when your finances are likely to become challenging. Economic swings may cause harm, including the 3rd Chinese month (4 Apr. - 4 May), the 5th Chinese month (5 Jun. - 5 Jul.), and the 8th Chinese month (7 Sep. - 7 Oct.) and the 11th month of China (6 Dec. '24 - 4 Jan. '25). Don't put yourself at danger by getting engaged in or investing in unlawful enterprises. Because there may be a criminal investigation.

Family

This year's family horoscope features favorable energy. At home, there is the option of preparing an auspicious event, acquiring expensive property, or recruiting new members. However, you must exercise caution since an unfortunate force from an evil star is on its way to annoy you. As a result, you should be cautious of persons in the house who are in dispute with those around. Be wary of subordinates or children destroying or stealing things in secret. The 3rd Chinese month (4 Apr. - 4 May), the 5th Chinese month (5 Jun. - 5 Jul.), the 8th Chinese month (7 Sep. - 7 Oct.), and the 11th Chinese month (6 Dec. '24 - 4 Jan. '25) are the months when family issues will arise.

Love

This year is fairly good in terms of love. The sky parted on the side. If you are still single, you will find the appropriate person. This year is said to be the ideal moment to ask for love or to propose. It is a fantastic moment since the skies are inclined to grant your love request. There are also favorable seasons for those of you planning an engagement or marriage. However, there will be periods during the year when your love will be frail. There will very certainly be quarrels and arguments during the 3rd Chinese month (4 Apr. - 4 May), the 5th Chinese month (5 Jun. - 5 Jul.), the 8th Chinese month (7 Sep. - 7 Oct.), and the 11th Chinese month (6 Dec. '24 - 4 Jan '25). You should be cautious with your remarks that produce displeasure with one another, since this will lead to division. Furthermore, do not intervene or act as a third party in other people's love and family ties. You should also avoid attending to places of amusement. Because it will bring an infinite number of issues..

Health

Your health is still important to the senior fortune teller this year. Because there will be issues with congenital disorders and difficulties. As a result, you should see your doctor on time, take your medication on time, and get adequate rest and sleep. In the interest of young people's health If you have to work hard, you will have no issues because your body is still robust. Full of strength and stamina, capable of overcoming difficult tasks. However, you should not overwork.

Year of the RABBIT (Gold) | (1951) & (2011)

"The RABBIT in the House" is a person born in the year of the RABBIT at the age of 73 years (1951) and 13 years (2011)

Overview

Because the planet that orbits into your house of destiny this year is "Jimui," this year is regarded fortunate and it is a delight that there will be a dinner in your home for people born in the Year of the Rabbit, around the age of 73. Gathering with family or hosting an auspicious celebration for children and grandkids. The house will get favorable power this year. Have the requirements for receiving both riches and gold. The stars have a high social rank and position. However, you cannot disregard the risk because in your house of destiny, a collection of bad stars is orbiting together to bother you, including the "Guangji star" and

"Pua Pai star," which the influence of these two stars will send. As a result, there will be disagreements and squabbles. Unexpected interfering events occur in the family, and one should be cautious of mishaps both at work and when traveling. As a result, you must exercise extreme caution and pay close attention.

The planets that move into their destiny house this year for the child's destiny around the age of 13 are "Dao Ngek Tung" because it has discovered the power of auspicious patronage to assist it. As a result, you may aid to propel your academics this year in the right path. Capable of scoring at the top of the class in tests, but what is concerning for children at this age is that there are likely to be quarrels over the year, or they may be bullied by classmates, or they may get into difficulty with other groups of friends. As a result, parents must exercise caution. If a youngster joins a group and has difficulties with other schools, they should figure out how to end it. Because it poses a risk of damage and eventual loss, resulting in misery. As a result, establishing friends with children. You should provide advise to avoid unpleasant surprises.

Career and Business

This year is a terrific time for senior destinies in jobs and enterprises to search for dependable heirs or grandkids to assist continue on the task. Taking care of new investments, in particular, will considerably boost investment efficiency. This year's studies must emphasize increased diligence for those destined for childcare. Avoid being distracted by outside stimuli that can easily cause you to lose concentration. The months in which education and work-trade grow and thrive include the 2nd Chinese month (5 Mar. - 3 Apr.) and the 6th Chinese month (6 Jul. - 6 Aug.), 9th Chinese month (8 Oct. - 6 Nov.) and 10th Chinese month (7 Nov. - 5 Dec.)

For starting a new career, investing in stocks, and making other types of investments. It met the requirements for deceit this year. As a result, you must first consider carefully.

Because the majority of them are dug and baited traps. The investment was not proposed with the best of intentions. As a result, please don't be so self-centered and greedy that you become a victim of a cheater. Especially during the 3rd Chinese month (4 Apr. - 4 May), the 5th Chinese month (5 Jun. - 5 Jul.), the 8th Chinese month (7 Sep. - 7 Oct.), and the 11th Chinese month (6 Dec '24 - 4 Jan '25). Furthermore, you must be wary of slaves that cause troubles and discomfort.

Financial

Overall, the financial fortunes of this year appear to be favorable. There will be additional money. However, there will be interference and asset loss in issues that you did not anticipate. As a result, you must take careful care of your working capital. Spending should be properly planned. Because if you are reckless, you are entitled to a financial crisis and a shortage of money. Especially during the months of the third Chinese month (4 Apr.- 4 May), the 5th Chinese month (5 Jun. - 5 Jul.), and the 8th Chinese month (7 Sep. - 7 Oct.) and the 11th month of China (6 Dec. '24 - 4 Jan '25). Make no loans or financial commitments. Both should avoid gambling. As for the months where income will continue to flow in and there will be good luck in the windfall, include the 2nd Chinese month (5 Mar. - 3 Apr.), the 6th Chinese month (6 Jul. - 6 Aug.). ,9th Chinese month (8 Oct. - 6 Nov.) and 10th Chinese month (7 Nov. - 5 Dec.).

Family

This year's family horoscope is a mixed bag. You should be more concerned about the safety of others in your home. Be wary of folks in your hometown when it comes to unexpected events. Keep an eye out for minors who are making trouble. However, you are still fortunate throughout the year. An auspicious star will arrive in the sky to assist, halving the intensity of the disaster. However, you should exercise caution during the months when your family may experience issues and upheaval, such as the 3rd Chinese month (4 Apr. - 4 May), the 5th Chinese month (5 Jun. - 5 Jul.), the 8th Chinese month (7 Sep. - 7 Oct.) and the 11th Chinese month (6 Dec. '24 - 4 Jan. '25). Allow minor things to generate conflict until it becomes a rift. You should also be wary of persons in the residence who are having disagreements with their neighbors. Destroying a long-standing friendship.

Love
There was no significant change in love and relationships among the seniors. Love is still going well. As a result, you should keep this connection going for a long period. Children, who frequently have worried and inquisitive minds, should be sternly admonished to practice control and to never have sex before getting married. Especially during the months when you should be extra alert and cautious, such as the 3rd Chinese month (4 Apr. - 4 May), the 5th Chinese month (5 Jun. - 5 Jul.), and the 8th Chinese month (7 Sep. - 7 Oct.) and the 11th Chinese month (6 Dec. '24 - 4 Jan. '25). You should avoid getting engaged in other people's families as a senior. Avoid disagreements and confrontations. For youngsters, be wary of being duped into falling in love and having regrets as a result.

Health

The overall picture of elder health will be better this year than previous. Because he benefited from the favorable stars that orbited the mansion of destiny. As a consequence, you will see a good doctor, good drugs, and a strategy for treating the ailment that you are this year. However, there are seasons of the year when you should be cautious. However, you must pay more attention to your health during the 3rd Chinese month (4 Apr. - 4 May), the 5th Chinese month (5 Jun. - 5 Jul.), the 8th Chinese month (7 Sep. - 7 Oct.), and the 7th Chinese month (6 Dec. '24 - 4 Jan. '25).

Year of the RABBIT (Water) | (1963)

" The Dharma rabbit" is a person born in the year of the RABBIT at the age of 61 years (1963)

Overview

This year is considered an auspicious year for you since the planet that orbits into your destiny house is Ngek Tung. Because they received riches, dividends, profits, and patronage power. Work will continue, and business will expand more smoothly than previous year. This year, you might search for heirs or assistance to join the firm and help it grow in the future. So you may extend your wings, grow your firm, branch out, or invest in a new venture. To establish a firm foundation for your children and grandkids, or to improve your financial situation in order to become more successful. The difficulties and challenges of the previous year will serve as lessons for this year, preventing you from repeating the same mistakes again. However, during the year, one should not overlook the bad stars that will circle and disrupt both the Guang Ji and Heng Sua stars. All of this will cause you troubles in a variety of areas. As a result, you should work rapidly to resolve any issues that have occurred and persisted until this year. Don't allow it get so huge that it's impossible to heal. You should also be wary of family members that are envious and have arguments. As an adult, you must be fair to all parties. Instead of choosing who you love, select who you despise. Whoever is correct, speak what is correct. Going the wrong route is wrong. There will be no disagreements that will disrupt the household's serenity.

Career and Business

In terms of work, this year is an excellent criteria. Work will go smoothly. Business will grow and flourish. Because they have clientele to back them up. You should cultivate connections within your business as well as with consumers and partners. Then, in order to achieve your objectives, concentrate on growing your business. As you can see, your business will grow and flourish. Especially during the months when your work and business will be prosperous, such as the 2nd Chinese month (5 Mar. - 3 Apr.), the 6th Chinese month (6 Jul. - 6 Aug.), the 9th Chinese month (8 Oct. - 6 Nov.) and the 10th Chinese month (7 Nov. - 5 Dec.). Furthermore, it is seen to be a suitable time to select an heir to assist with the task. can take over the task as a representative to carry it on in the future. Which, at your age, will only cause you to move backwards by putting too much stress on your health, or you can accomplish it but the outcomes aren't as excellent as they should be. If you are willing to have your children come and share the load. It will produce a lot of good work. As a result, the labor should be handed on to the children and grandkids, who will begin to assist.

For the months when work and business may face barriers and troubles, such as the 3rd Chinese month (4 Apr. - 4 May), the 5th Chinese month (5 Jun. - 5 Jul.), the 8th Chinese month (7 Sep. - 7 Oct.), and the 11th Chinese month (6 Dec. '24 - 4 Jan. '25). Be wary of subordinates who embezzle, corrupt, or do harm. Be cautious while signing labor contracts. If you are not cautious, you may fall prey to deception.

Financial

In terms of financial luck, this year will be better than previous. The money will come in from a variety of sources, depending on what you have already invested. The 2nd Chinese month (5 Mar. - 3 Apr.), the 6th Chinese month (6 Jul. - 6 Aug.), the 9th Chinese month (8 Oct. c. - 6 Nov.), and the 10th month of China (7 Nov. - 5 Dec.) have exceptional financial luck and success. However, there will be current costs that will suck money out of your wallet or you may discover a money leak. Capital If you have not prepared by saving money. A lack of liquidity might be an issue.

You must exercise caution during the following months, which will be particularly disruptive to your finances: the third month of China (4 April - 4 May), the fifth month of China (5 June - 5 July), and the eighth month. China (7 Sept. - 7 Oct.) and the 11th month of China (6 Dec. '24 - 4 Jan. '25). Do not be greedy or swayed into investing in illicit businesses. Because you may not be able to avoid the criminal crime and will have to pay a large punishment. Gambling is also forbidden. Do not lend money or sign any form of financial promise to anyone.

Family

This year's family fortunes are not going well. It was due to the wicked stars Guang Ji and Ng Suo's influence, who were attacking the family

basis. As a result, you must exercise greater caution in the event of an unforeseen mishap. Be cautious of accidents that may occur among members of the household. Keep an eye out for family members arguing and injuring one other. Specifically, the 3rd Chinese month (4 April - 4 May), the 5th Chinese month (5 June - 5 July), the 8th Chinese month (7 Sep. - 7 Oct.), and the 11th month of China (6 Dec. '24 - 4 Jan. '25). Be wary of persons in the house wielding authority until they get into difficulties with government agencies or elsewhere. With powerful individuals spreading havoc across the home.
Avoid disagreements, disputes, and litigation with your neighbors.

.

Love
The destined person's love horoscope is regarded ordinary. You will be able to take your loved one on a trip to a faraway area or arrange a charitable event to benefit people in other places. However, if you enter the Chinese 3rd month (4 Apr. - 4 May), 5th Chinese month (5 Jun - 5 July), the 8th Chinese month (7 Sep. - 7

Oct.), and 11th Chinese month (6 Dec. '24 - 4 Jan. '25), be wary of disputes with your spouse next to you. Avoid going to entertainment establishments. Because it will generate strife in the family. Furthermore, do not meddle with other people's family connections during this time. You must also strengthen your thinking..

Health

The physical health of this year is deemed medium, neither good nor terrible. It all boils down to taking care of oneself. You will get sick at some point over the year. However, you will be fortunate to discover a good doctor, excellent medicine, and proper therapy that will ease or heal your condition in a short period of time. You should, however, take care of your relaxation and obtain adequate sleep. This will not result in the recurrence of the old ailment. The months in which you need to pay more attention to your health include the 3rd Chinese month (4 April - 4 May), the 5th Chinese month (5 June - 5 July), the 8th Chinese month. (7 Sep. - 7 Oct.) and the 11th Chinese month (6 Dec. '24 - 4 Jan. '25) should be careful about drinking and eating hygiene. If you notice any changes in your body, please visit a doctor right once. Things that were once heavy will become light. You should not drive if you are under the influence of alcohol or other intoxicants. Be cautious of roadside injuries..

Year of the RABBIT (Wood) | (1975)

" The RABBIT on the moon" is a person born in the year of the RABBIT at the age of 48 years (1975)

Overview

The star Ji Mui is the planet that rotates into your house of destiny this year during the Year of the Rabbit. This is an auspicious star that promotes, but this year may need you to raise a new flag, change your goals, and enhance your devotion and tenacity. Any labor activity still needs calm, prudence, and patience. To limit the flow of impediments since there will be issues with people who must interact with business. You will be hampered or harassed if you do not succumb to caution. This is due to the appearance of the wicked stars "Guang Ji" and "Dao Xiao Ying" during the year, which are circling to spread their lethal influence and infest the house of destiny. This year, you must exercise caution while using terms that may offend others. It can often result in quarrels at home or at the workplace, as well as an unforeseen vengeance event. Including concerns with accidents and the impacts of health conditions, such as heart disease, liver illness, or leg injuries. This causes impediments to the flow of labor and business, rendering it ineffective.

.

.

Career and Business

This year's work will be interrupted by monsoons at times. But there are times when happiness and tranquility appear. It is necessary to revise your change plan in order to keep up with the times. Build connections inside the agency to foster unity and concentrate on producing outcomes, speeding sales, and increasing profits. This year, if you enhance your diligence and wealth, you will be rewarded for your perseverance throughout the year. Please do not be disheartened by hurdles or allow excellent possibilities pass you by. The months in which your career and business will advance and prosper include the 2nd Chinese month (5 Mar. - 3 Apr.), the 6th Chinese month (6 Jul. - 6 Aug.), the 9th Chinese month (8 Oct. - 6 Nov.), and the 10th Chinese month (7 Nov. - 5 Dec.). The months in which business and trade problems and obstacles will arise including: 3rd Chinese month (4 Apr. – 4 May), 5th Chinese month (5 Jun. – 5 Jul.), 8th Chinese month (7 Sep. – 7 Oct.) and the 11th month of China (6 Dec. '24 - 4 Jan. '25) where activities must be circumspect since there will be fierce trade competitors. You must also be cautious that greed can cause you to fall victim to crooks. If there are conditions for signing various contracts at this time, you should carefully review them since there may be hidden downsides. Furthermore, minors or subordinates should be avoided for embezzlement, corruption, or destruction.

.

Financial

The budget for this year is modest. A normal flow of revenue exists for direct income from wage or from the sale of goods or services. However, windfall money is fraught with danger. You must avoid becoming greedy or greedy. Be wary of being a victim of others because of your own wants. You should be extra cautious, especially during the months when finances will falter and leaks will be discovered, such as the 3rd Chinese month (4 Apri. - 4 May), the 5th Chinese month (5 Jun. - 5 Jul.), the 8th Chinese month (7 Sep. - 7 Oct.) and the 11th Chinese month (6 Dec. '24 - 4 Jan. '25). Spending on entertainment should be kept to a minimum during this time period. Finally, don't squander money. It is also not permitted to lend money or sign financial promises to others. and sternly ban participation in unlawful business or copyright infringement. For the months when finances are flowing smoothly, they are the 2nd Chinese month (5 Mar. - 3 Apr.), the 6th Chinese month (6 Jul. - 6 Aug.), the 9th Chinese month (8 Oct. Jan. – 6

Nov.) and the 10th Chinese month (7 Nov. – 5 Dec.)

Family

Horoscope for your family If there is a criterion for conducting any auspicious activities at home this year, the auspicious power will boost the auspiciousness and bring only wonderful and happy things to pass. However, if no fortunate occurrence occurs at your house this year, you must look at the members of the house. There will be quarrels and quarrels inside the family or fights with neighbors, leading the family to be uneasy. The 3rd Chinese month (4 Apr. - 4 May) and the 5th Chinese month (5 Jun. - 5 Aug.) , the Chinese 8th month (7 Sep. - 7 Oct.) and the Chinese 11th month (6 Dec. '24 - 4 Jan.'25)are the months to be cautious of since troubles and confusion are more likely to develop in the home. Avoid arguing and advise others in the house not to do so. Going outdoors to show off your talents like a gangster since you could encounter something harsh and get in trouble. Also, keep an eye out for items that have been damaged, misplaced, or stolen..

Love

In terms of love and relationships, this year has been quite smooth. You will find a companion that adores you, looks after you, and is really supportive. You can engage in both local and international tourist vacations as well as volunteer to aid society or relieve public calamities.

However, there are some times of the year when love is particularly fragile and arguments are more likely, such as the 3rd Chinese month (4 Apr. - 4 May), the 5th Chinese month (5 Jun. - 5 Jul.), the 8th Chinese month (7 Sep. - 7 Oct.), and the 11th Chinese month (6 Dec. '24 - 4 Jan. '25), when you should be wary of problems with third parties interfering. Arguments developed regarding whether one should monitor one's own conduct so that one does not walk into entertainment places and become infected with sickness as a result..

.

Health

This year's health difficulties are not promising. You should be cautious about the recurrence of existing ailments, as well as liver and heart disease and limb difficulties. Furthermore, the fortune teller should be extra stringent this year and pay attention to food hygiene. You should watch your food, especially during the following months: 3rd Chinese month (4 Apr. - 4 May), 5th Chinese month (5 Jun. - 5 Jul.), 8th Chinese month (7 Sep. - 7 Oct.), and 11th Chinese month (6 Dec. '24 - 4 Jan. '25). Avoid eating too many sugary, salty, and fatty foods, and restrict your consumption of varied beverages. You should not drive after drinking beer or other intoxicants during a party. You should also be more careful about accidents during work. Don't be careless when traveling by road...

Year of the RABBIT (Fire) | (1987)

" The rabbit at the full moon" is a person born in the year of the RABBIT at the age of 37 years (1987)

Overview

For individuals born during the Year of the Rabbit, the planet that revolves into your house of destiny this year is the fortunate star Ji Mui, which orbits to promote. This year, however, you may need to create new goals, tweak existing ones, and boost your vigilance. Any labor activity still demands patience, prudence, and calm. In order to lessen the flow of impediments since there will be issues with individuals who must interact with business. You will be impeded or harassed if you do not succumb to caution. This is because the demonic stars "Guang Ji" and "Dao Xiao Ying" arrived throughout the year, spreading their fatal influence and infesting the house of destiny. This year, you must be cautious of words and phrases that may upset people without thinking, resulting in quarrels inside the house or company or unforeseen vengeance situations. Problems with accidents should be avoided, as should the impacts of health issues such as heart disease, liver illness, or limb injuries. This causes impediments to the flow of labor and business, rendering it ineffective.

Career and Business

This year's work will be interrupted by monsoons at times. But there are times when happiness and tranquility appear. It is necessary to revise your change plan in order to keep up with the times. Build relationships inside the agency to foster unity and cooperation. Concentrate on producing results, increasing sales, and increasing money. Wealth will be a reward for those who are determined this year if you enhance your diligence. Please do not be disheartened by barriers or miss out on wonderful possibilities this year.The months in which your career and business will progress and prosper include the 2nd Chinese month (5 Mar. - 3 Apr.), the 6th Chinese month (6 Jul. - 6 Aug.), the 9th Chinese month (8 Oct. - 6 Nov.) and the 10th Chinese month (7 Nov. - 5 Dec.) for the months when business and trade problems and obstacles will arise, including: 3rd Chinese month (4 Apr. – 4 May), 5th Chinese month (5 Jun. – 5 Jul.), 8th Chinese month (7 Sep. – 7 Oct.) and the 11th month of

China (6 Dec. 2024 - 4 Jan. 2025) where work must be done carefully. Because there will be tough commercial rivals. You must also be wary of falling victim to fraudsters due to greed. If there are conditions for signing various contracts at this time, you should carefully examine them since there may be hidden downsides. Furthermore, children or subordinates should be cautious of embezzlement, corruption, or destruction.

Financial

The budget for this year is minimal. The flow of revenue from salaries or the sale of goods or services is typical. However, windfall money is fraught with danger. You must avoid becoming greedy or greedy. Be wary of being a victim of others because of your own wants. You should be extra cautious, particularly during the months when finances will suffer and leaks may be discovered, including 3rd Chinese month (4 Apr. - 4 May), the 5th Chinese month (5 June - 5 July), the 8th Chinese month (7 Sep. - 7 Oct) and 11th Chinese month (6 Dec '24 - 4 Jan '25). Be cautious with your expenditures during this time. The cost of entertainment should be kept to a minimum. Don't throw it away. It is highly unlawful to lend money to others or sign financial assurances, and it is also strongly forbidden to engage in criminal business or violation of intellectual property rights. They are the 2nd Chinese month (5 Mar. - 3 Apr.), the 6th Chinese month (6 Jul. - 6 Aug.), the 9th Chinese month (8 Oct. - 6 Nov.), and the 10th Chinese month (7 Nov. - 5 Dec.).

Family

Horoscope for your family If there is a criterion for conducting any auspicious activities at home this year, the auspicious power will boost the auspiciousness and bring only wonderful and happy things to pass. However, if no fortunate occurrence occurs at your house this year, you must look at the members of the house. There will be quarrels and quarrels inside the family, as well as fights with neighbors, leading the family to be uneasy. Be wary of arguments during the 3rd Chinese month (4 Apr. - 4 May), the 5th Chinese month (5 Jun. - 5 Jul.), the 8th Chinese month (7 Sep. - 7 Oct.), and the 11th Chinese month (6 Dec. '24 - 4 Jan. '25). Warn folks in the home not to behave like gangsters and go outside to show off their talents since they could come across something difficult and get in trouble. Also, keep an eye out for items that have been damaged, misplaced, or stolen.

Love

In terms of love, relationships this year are very straightforward; you will find your spouse, lover, compassionate, and helpful. Both local and international tourist vacations are available, as is volunteering to improve society or relieve public calamities. However, there are some times of the year when love is quite fragile and arguments can easily occur, such as the 3rd Chinese month (4 Apr. - 4 May.), the 5th Chinese month (5 Jun - 5 Jul.), the 8th Chinese month (7 Sep. - 7 Oct.), and the 11th Chinese month (6 Dec. '24 - 4 Jan. '25), when you should be cautious of problems with third parties interfering. There was debate regarding whether one should monitor one's own behavior in order to avoid being dumb and wandering into areas of fun. Because you may be infected with sickness as an added benefit.

Health

This year, your physical health may suffer from several ailments. If you wish to strengthen your body and improve your immunity. You must workout for 30 minutes every day. This will aid in the strengthening of your immune system. The 3rd Chinese month (4 Apr. - 4 May), the 5th Chinese month (5 Jun. - 5 Jul.), the 8th Chinese month (7 Sep.- 7 Oct.), and the 11th Chinese month (6 Dec. '24 - 4 Jan. '25) are all important months for your health. Please be mindful of your eating habits.

Chinese Astrology Horoscope for Each Month

Month 12 in the Tiger Year (6 Jan 24 - 3 Feb 24)

As we enter this month, the path of people born in the Year of the Rabbit has become rocky, with ups and downs. The prerequisites for destiny are an easy start and a challenging finish, which makes the journey exceedingly unpredictable. What you should do this month is having the fortitude to make decisions if any events come your way. If a destructive error has already occurred, you must dare to accept responsibility rather than hide it so that the situation does not snowball into a major issue. In terms of work and business this month, be wary of the consequences of subordinates splitting up or resigning. You must convince with honesty and positive sentiments so that the agency does not lose excellent resources. Furthermore, this is another month in which you must visit and deepen ties with folks you normally contact on a regular basis. Customers or business partners that defect and change their minds about using your services should be avoided. This is due to a lengthy period of distance in the relationship, as well as a lack of excellent engagement with partners, clients, or other individuals with whom one must communicate.

This pay is typical direct income in terms of fortune. Windfall gaming money poses a high amount of risk. Rather than becoming greedy, the greatest way is to avoid it. If you invest in an unlawful enterprise, you will not only lose money, but you may also wind up in prison.

This month brings about family harmony. It is still smooth in terms of affection, with no storm waves. Single people who are sincerely in love and expect to marry this month have the right to be soft-hearted toward their sweetheart. You will all find fulfillment whether you ask for love or reconciliation. There is no cause for alarm in terms of normal physical health.

Support Days: 4 Jan., 8 Jan., 12 Jan., 16 Jan., 20 Jan., 24 Jan., 28 Jan.
Lucky Days: 11 Jan., 23 Jan.
Misfortune Days: 10 Jan., 22 Jan.
Bad Days: 5 Jan., 7 Jan., 17 Jan., 19 Jan., 29 Jan, 31 Jan.

Month 1 in the Rabbit Year (4 Feb 24 - 5 Mar 24)

This month marks the start of the Chinese New Year. When it comes to this year, horoscopes for persons born in the Year of the Rabbit are available. It may be said to be a great time. Overall, the conditions are to be highly diligent and to receive a lot of riches. As a result, in order to have more money at this excellent time of year. As a result, you should utilize the blunders of the previous year as lessons and experiences to figure out how to prevent making the same destructive mistakes in the future. You should do anything on this occasion: arrange finances. Human resources organize activities in accordance with the circumstances. Building excellent relationships with individuals you have to deal with is one of them. The engine may be increased to full speed when the proper moment arrives.

This month is a month of progress in terms of work and business. You can opt to invest in a variety of enterprises, such as branch expansion or increased investments in new trade marketplaces. Because fantastic possibilities like this do not come around very frequently, so do not pass up this precious opportunity. Be dedicated to your work. You will witness worthwhile outcomes.

Because they meet the power of a pleasant companion, the family's fortunes are tranquil and smooth. The heart represents the loving side. Those of you who are still unmarried will have charm and the opportunity to fall in love with the right person. But first, please take the time to get to know each other. Don't rush into making a decision.

Overall health is still excellent. You should, however, boost your body's rest. Don't be so focused on getting money that you don't take time to rest or care for yourself.

Support Days: 1 Feb., 5 Feb., 9 Feb., 13 Feb., 17 Feb., 21 Feb., 25 Feb., 29 Feb.
Lucky Days: 4Feb., 16 Feb., 28 Feb
Misfortune Days: 3 Feb., 15 Feb., 27 Feb.
Bad Days: 10 Feb., 12 Feb., 22 Feb., 24 Feb

Month 2 in the Rabbit Year (6 Mar 24 - 5 Apr 24)
Your horoscope born in the Year of the Rabbit enters this month and moves to the line of partnership that enhances power. It also gets fortunate rays from the "Dao Ji Mui" and "Dao Leng Tek" circling to light in the center of the home, showing the way to wealth once again. Obstacles and issues that have gathered and caused concern will be addressed, and you will be able to stroll down a smooth route. This month, you should have the bravery to pursue possibilities while being diligent and determined to attain your goal.

There will be plenty of prospects for promotion at work. Businesses will flourish and grow. When the tide comes in, you should scoop it as soon as possible. Furthermore, when paired with dedication and commitment, you will be able to push your task until it meets its objectives. There will be strong chances for anyone doing business this month in a variety of areas. There is a probability that the product may be well received, become a market leader, or establish a reputation in some way. You can also join joint venture stocks or invest in other firms that interest you. Don't allow this great opportunity pass you by without doing something to capitalize on it.

This salary horoscope is in a good financial situation. When there is revenue, money still pours in. You should still save and handle your money wisely.

The family side of things is still running nicely and routinely. Furthermore, throughout this time, families and friends are all helpful and encouraging. If you have any issues, you will receive excellent assistance.

On the plus side, the love tree blooms and yields exquisite fruit. The body is in good health. This is due to the fact that there are only joyful things, hence there is nothing to cause the mind to suffer. The body recovers when the mind is at rest.

Support Days: 4 Mar., 8 Mar., 12 Mar., 16 Mar., 20 Mar., 24 Mar., 28 Mar.
Lucky Days: 11 Mar., 23 Mar.
Misfortune Days: 10 Mar., 22 Mar.
Bad Days: 5 Mar., 7 Mar., 17 Mar., 19 Mar., 29 Mar., 31 Mar.

Month 3 in the Rabbit Year (6 Apr 24 - 5 May 24)
The road of life for those born in the Year of the Rabbit this month is moving into a negative direction. Therefore, it is impossible to predict that the situation may change at any time. There is a chance that there will be big obstacles in your work. Be careful when trading as there will be competitors coming in to take market share. What you should do on this occasion is not to interfere in other people's work. Do your own duties well. Always maintain good relationships with people both at the top and bottom.

Monsoons will disrupt your job and business at this time. Signing contracts or other paperwork gives you the right to be taken advantage of. You will face disagreements inside the company or issues with the people you must deal with. As a result, I urge that you maintain a nice demeanor and cultivate positive connections with your coworkers and people around you in order to assist with the operation. Business interaction is easy.

This salary forecast is faltering and becoming stuck. As a result, avoid excessive spending and avoid gambling or trying your luck in any way. Furthermore, do not lend money or sign financial assurances to others. Because you may suffer as a result of something you did not do.

There is pandemonium among the household. You should take extra precautions and pay special attention to the safety and health of your family members. Be wary of youngsters or slaves who cause mischief and harm.

Love has no positive or bad aspects. Relationships continue to function normally. But you must continue to bring love and tenderness. Always look after the other person. So that love does not fade

Be cautious of liver illness, heart disease, and unforeseen accidents at this time.

In terms of establishing a new career, investing in stocks, and other sectors. You should be wary of being duped. Before making an investment decision, you should thoroughly analyze all considerations.

.

Support Days: 1 Apr., 5 Apr., 9 Apr., 13 Apr., 17 Apr., 21 Apr., 25 Apr., 29 Apr.
Lucky Days: 4 Apr., 16 Apr., 28 Apr
Misfortune Days: 3 Apr., 15 Apr., 27 Apr
Bad Days: 10 Apr., 12 Apr., 22 Apr., 24 Apr.

Month 4 in the Rabbit Year (6 May 24 - 5 Jun 24)
The horoscope of people born in the Year of the Rabbit is optimistic as we enter this month. The majority of issues and roadblocks have been fixed and removed. This month, you should do the following: Knowing how to capitalize on

favorable opportunities to make up for lost time. This month, you must have the confidence to develop your firm or make further investments. Whether it's branching out, extending your field of business, speeding your job, or growing sales in the internet world to go forward and achieve your objectives.

In terms of work, especially commerce, you will receive fortunate energy from the good stars. To be valuable, you must change and fix your mistakes. As a result, you should be more cautious. To achieve your objective, move forward and work to the best of your ability. Furthermore, many things are moving in the correct way at this time. You can start a new career, invest in shares with others, or invest in a previously planned target firm. You only need to have the bravery to establish your own business or to invest and go further. Under the auspicious and peaceful force that encourages. This month is thus an excellent opportunity for you to gain significant profits.

This wage fortune is plentiful. Money comes in from a variety of sources as a result of what you have sown. You will harvest what you sow. However, you should continue to work hard this month if you want to make a livelihood. Always strive to improve oneself in order to stay up with the fast changing environment. The more you grow as a person. The likelihood of receiving riches will rise in lockstep.

This month, favorable energy will be discovered inside the family. People in the home will bring you excellent news. There may be guidelines for dealing with fortunate events. or new members have been added.

This month's love relationships are calm and usual. As a result, this is a fantastic time to plan a trip with your companion.
In terms of health, avoid injuries and bleeding caused by tools or equipment. You should also be cautious of accidents caused by driving on the road.

Support Days: 3 May., 7 May., 11 May., 15 May., 19 May., 23 May., 27 May., and 31 May
Lucky Days: 10 May., 22 May.
Misfortune Days: 9 May., 21 May.
Bad Days: 4 May., 6 May., 16 May., 18 May., 28 May., 30 May

Month 5 in the Rabbit Year (6 Jun 24 - 6 Jul 24)
This month, your fate will shift from front to rear. The houses of the zodiac travel vertically. What you should be wary of are health issues, ailments caused by hidden threats that may stymie your career growth. As a result, this month, you should prioritize your health. Several difficulties are stalled during this time period. You should talk to an adult or a guru who has expertise guiding the way in order to help each other overcome the crisis and the problem and discover a light at the end of the tunnel.

This salary will have an unanticipated incident that will break and injure you. Furthermore, revenue has declined. However, expenditures lurk in the shadows. As a result, anything that can be preserved should be saved first in order to keep the system liquid. Furthermore, do not add to your obligations by investing in windfalls, gambling, or calculating your luck in any form of stock lottery. This includes forbidding individuals from lending money or writing commitments to assist others.

During this time, the work and trading environment is similarly hectic. Contacting consumers or business partners will be difficult. It will be simpler to reach your goals if you enhance your communication abilities.

There is still nothing to be concerned about within the family. This month will see a lot of heart changes in terms of love and relationships. You must modify your conduct, which frequently causes your mind to wander. Be wary of unwittingly starting fights and developing rifts in the family.

In terms of health, avoid getting sick as a result of heavy effort. You should also be cautious about recurring gastritis and intestinal illness. Starting a new career, buying stocks, and investing in other industries are all options. The outlook for this month is bleak. To acquire a foothold, please avoid or withdraw; it will be safer.

Support Days: 4 Jun., 8 Jun., 10 Jun., 12 Jun., 16 Jun., 20 Jun., 24 Jun., 28 Jun.
Lucky Days: 3 Jun., 15 Jun. ., 27 Jun
Misfortune Days: 2 Jun., 14 Jun., 26 Jun.
Bad Days: 9 Jun., 11 Jun., 21 Jun., 23 Jun.

Month 6 in the Rabbit Year (7 Jul 24 - 7 Aug 24)

This month, your fortune has changed for the better. This is due to the fact that the zodiac houses migrate to coincide with the months in which they are partners. When you have the promotion month's backing and the rays of the fortunate stars that convey energy, the direction of your horoscope has the capacity to fly upwards. This month, you should work on improving your interpersonal skills and maintaining courtesy and respect. When communicating with consumers or business partners, listen more and grasp their genuine requirements. To minimize self-perception and aid in harm reduction. Always prepare yourself, your ideas, your staff, and your work procedures for fresh rounds of funding or expansion. You may need to have a backup plan in place to avoid repeating the same error.

There will be a test point in terms of employment and business during this era. As a result, you must carefully prioritize your tasks. You should also prepare for potential situations and wait and observe what happens before taking any action. To avoid making a costly mistake, avoid being hasty.

This wage fortune is average. However, you must still plan your expenditures very carefully. You cannot compromise on diligence, and you must not be disheartened by hurdles. There is a potential to acquire additional wealth as a result. The family fortune is serene and orderly.

On the romantic front, it is a moment when the sky is clear and brilliant. People you care about are attentive and take excellent care of you. In terms of your health, keep an eye out for excessive blood pressure. Work-related stress frequently prevents you from sleeping. Be cautious, since it will result in a variety of ailments.

Starting a new career, buying stocks, and investing in other industries are all options. This month, the mood is upbeat. You have the option of investing.

Support Days: 2 Jul., 6 Jul., 10 Jul., 14 Jul., 18 Jul., 22 Jul., 26 Jul., 30 Jul.
Lucky Days: 9 Jul., 21 Jul.
Misfortune Days: 8 Jul., 20 Jul.
Bad Days: 3 Jul., 5 Jul., 15 Jul., 17 Jul., 27 Jul., 29 Jul

Month 7 in the Rabbit Year (8 Aug 24 - 7 Sep 24)
This month, people born in the Year of the Rabbit have a difficult route to adulthood. The zodiac house travels to meet the opposition line, causing the horoscope's course to fall. Work and business will be difficult. You must also be mindful of major issues that may arise and render you unable to sit still.

There will be a risky trade checkpoint. Both will face conflicts in the administrative line. Be wary of clients or business partners that defect and choose services from rivals. In this instance, you will need to change your plan, beginning with yourself, in order to recover confidence. In addition to signing any contract paperwork. You must be alert. Don't let a minor leak create huge damage.

Financially, this month is still the benchmark for leakage and loss. You should carefully arrange your spending. To avoid stumbling and becoming caught till you can't reach your front or back. The fortune remains unknown. As a result, you should avoid taking risks in order to avoid being injured.

The family horoscope for this month is not favorable. Take precautions for your own and your family's safety. Be especially cautious of the potential for injury and bleeding from equipment and appliances. You must also be cautious of potential robbers.

The love horoscope for this month creates waves and breezes that are simple to offend. Look past the little details, and the wind and waves will quiet down just fine.

Be wary of infectious illnesses and outbreaks in terms of health. You should focus more on eating hygiene.

Starting a new career, entering stocks, and investing in other industries are all options for family and friends. This month has been nothing but horrible. You should maintain your distance..

Support Days: 3 Aug., 7 Aug., 11 Aug., 15 Aug., 19 Aug., 23 Aug., 27 Aug., 31 Aug.
Lucky Days: 2 Aug., 14 Aug., 26 Aug
Misfortune Days: 1 Aug., 13 Aug., 25 Aug.
Bad Days: 8 Aug., 10 Aug., 20 Aug., 22 Aug.

Month 8 in the Rabbit Year (8 Sep 24 - 7 Oct 24)

The fate conditions for people born in the Year of the Rabbit this month show that they will have half pleasant and half terrible experiences. Working or engaging in numerous tasks cannot be done carelessly or impatiently. It will result in errors and damage that you will have to repair later. What you should do this month is: If a quarrel happens, please follow the rules of gentleness and tranquility, and should not favor one side over another.

This salary horoscope may cause you to lose assets. Financial leakage and unanticipated costs will occur. As a result, you should first organize your budget and spend wisely. You should also avoid gambling. Engage in no illicit enterprise or tax evasion. Because the hand of the law may come after you this month.

In terms of employment and business, you must be wary of confrontations during this time. Conflicts between insiders and the internal work system will produce chaos by interfering with others' work. It makes managing work difficult and gives you a headache. As a result, please assist your task and do your best in accordance with your obligations.

This month has been rather hectic in the household. You must be cautious about people in the house trespassing or having problems with other people, which might spread an event and impact the people in the house.

The love horoscope phase is as enjoyable as the honeymoon period. As a result, it is appropriate to take your loved one on a sightseeing vacation to improve the bond.

It appears to be in good health. However, you must still be cautious about seasonal ailments, viral disorders, and food poisoning.

Starting a new career, buying stocks, and investing in other industries are all options. This month's timing is not ideal.

Support Days: 4 Sep., 8 Sep., 12 Sep., 16 Sep., 20 Sep., 24 Sep., 28 Sep.
Lucky Days: 7 Sep, 20 Sep.
Misfortune Days: 7 Sep, 20 Sep.
Bad Days: 6 Sep, 19 Sep, 30 Sep.

Month 9 in the Rabbit Year (8 Oct 24 - 6 Nov 24)
This month's horoscope for people born in the Year of the Rabbit. The path of life has come to an end at the alliance line. The fortunate stars "Ji Mui" and "Jiang Chae" were discovered immediately sparkling and sending auspicious energy to support the house's fate. As a result, the auspicious light of the stars serves to encourage and promote easy work and profitable company. You should endeavor this

month to create and improve relationships in the workplace so that you can work together to finish a large task. You must rely on the strength of unity and the support of others to propel you forward. Your work is successful and moving forward.

Salary fortune: This is a really favorable period for money to come in and go out in a variety of ways. There will be significant cash streams from your investment. May you be more diligent and determined to improve yourself in order to put more money in your pocket.

Work, including trade, is blessed by Dao Dee Songserm. As a result, working during this time is like being on turbo, allowing you to get at your objective faster than normal. Those who work this month have the option of being promoted to a higher position and receiving a pay raise. It is a good moment to be in business. You may opt to invest in the previously planned target business. Because now is a fantastic moment for the surroundings to be peaceful and smooth. It also has favorable promotional power. Don't leave the treasure cave with nothing in your hands.

Patronage reigns supreme throughout the household. There are still wonderful tales and triumphs to share and celebrate in the house. In terms of love, the sky favors you this month, pointing to birds as birds and sticks as wood.

Everyone is in good physical condition. When you feel content and at ease. Physical health is also beneficial..

Support Days: 2 Oct., 6 Oct., 10 Oct., 14 Oct., 18 Oct., 22 Oct., 26 Oct., 30 Oct.
Lucky Days: 1 Oct., 13 Oct., 25 Oct
Misfortune Days: 12 Oct., 24 Oct.
Bad Days: 7 Oct., 9 Oct., 19 Oct., 21 Oct., 31 Oct.

Month 10 in the Rabbit Year (7 Nov 24 - 6 Dec 24)
The horoscope of people born in the Year of the Rabbit has a better trajectory as we enter this

month. However, the challenges and impediments have not fully vanished. On this occasion, you should cultivate and deepen positive ties with those around you. Customers, business partners, and those with whom you are constantly in contact, both inside and outside the corporation. Despite the fact that I have not requested assistance at this time. However, certain things will go more smoothly.

In terms of job and business at this time, even if there may be difficulties and issues to overcome. However, you will encounter customers eager to assist you. As a result, may the Lord of Destiny multiply your diligence and dedication. On the one hand, work quickly to repair and improve the job. The opposing party must go forward and strive toward the goals established for future advancement.

This wage fortune is bearable. There will be returns even if you invest a particular amount of money. It is thought to be worthwhile to make the investment. However, there is one thing the fortune teller should avoid: gambling, which will only result in catastrophic losses.

There is harmony and fortunate power of support inside the family. Family members have bright, cheerful grins. Family and friends are all encouraging. You will make good friends and be honest with one another.

When it comes to love, pleasant partnerships

There were no big health issues to be concerned about.

Starting a new career, buying stocks, and investing in other industries are all options. You must still use caution. Because crooks are still seeking for methods to get in and exploit you.

.

Support Days: 3 Nov., 7 Nov., 11 Nov., 15 Nov., 19 Nov., 23 Nov., 27 Nov.
Lucky Days: 6 Nov., 18 Nov., 30 Nov
Misfortune Days: 5 Nov., 17 Nov., 29 Nov

Bad Days: 2 Nov., 12 Nov., 114 Nov., 24 Nov., 26 Nov.

Month 11 in the Rabbit Year (7 Dec 24 - 5 Jan 25)

This month, your fortunes have once again turned negative. Because the house of Zodiac arrived near the conflict line, they were met with a great number of malevolent stars orbiting the community. Causing the horoscope's path to shift, causing work to become difficult and business to suffer from monsoon waves. During this month, avoid doing anything that interferes with the tasks of others. Also, don't act as if you don't care about other people. Be wary of envious persons who will try to intimidate you.

This is a little wage. You will also encounter unforeseen bills that drain your bank account. As a result, avoid gambling. Do not lend money or sign financial promises on behalf of others. Be cautious not to get engaged in illegal activities or engage in tax evasion business to fool officials, as this will become an issue and result in property loss.

In terms of employment, this month was a significant challenge. Every endeavor is fraught with danger, especially unresolved internal disputes. Another source of concern is the wolf in sheep's clothing, who will come to mislead and fool others. We must be cautious not to be misled by greed. It will cause you to easily lose your position. Furthermore, several contracts are being made. You should thoroughly inspect it.

There was still upheaval inside the household. This month, you should focus on home security and keep an eye out for missing or stolen goods.

You should be cautious about falling astray in love. It will cause strife and may infect you with sexually transmitted illnesses.

In terms of health, keep an eye out for liver issues and traffic hazards.

This month is not ideal for starting a new career, buying stocks, or investing. You may have to postpone or refrain.

Support Days: 1 Dec., 5 Dec., 9 Dec., 13 Dec., 17 Dec., 21 Dec., 25 Dec., 29 Dec.
Lucky Days: 12 Dec., 24 Dec.
Misfortune Days: 11 Dec., 23 Dec.
Bad Days: 6 Dec., 8 Dec., 18 Dec., 20 Dec., 30 Dec.

Amulet for The Year of the RABBIT

"Octagonal Sign of the Swan Dragon to ward off misfortune"

This year, those born in the Year of the Rabbit should set up and worship spiritual things. "Octagonal Dragon Swan Sign to ward off misfortune" to improve your luck. Put it on your work desk or cash register to keep you safe. Keep your cool and your spirits up. The task being done is making progress and prospering. It also helps to bless the business so that it runs smoothly and successfully. Money pours in and grows, offering the ruler of destiny peace and tranquillity.

It is claimed that people are part of the life on our planet. They are regulated by the rules of the cosmos, which are made up of cyclical symbols representing the 12 zodiac signs and the elements. Can be separated into two types: "ten branches of the sky" and "twelve branches of the earth." The 10 sky branches will reflect the influence of the universe's strength, which is tied to the 5 elements and 4 directions on the compass disc, while the 12 earth stalks are related to the 12 zodiac signs. During these 12 years of life, there will be both friends who promote and adversaries who destroy one another. The whole 12-year period will center around causing both merit and demerit.

Those born in the Year of the Rabbit or Mia believe their fate lies in the zodiac sign Bao. Even if money will spread this year, your fortune is unpredictable. However, the costs are also quite significant. You should make an effort to save money and diversify your investments. Work may quickly lead to disagreements and fights. You should lessen your prejudice. Don't be overly opinionated, and increase your diligence to ensure that things go well. Love may be isolating. You must intentionally regulate your emotions if you do not wish to separate ways. Concerning your health, be aware that overworking will render you bedridden. If you want to solve an issue, you should surround yourself with sacred things and wear auspicious pendants. "Octagonal Dragon and Swan Sign to Ward Off Misfortune" to aid in job advancement, lucrative business, and increasing income. Stay away from disasters and other disruptive situations.

"The 8-sided Dragon and Swan sign wards off misfortune" The front has fortunate symbols on it. "Dragon pair of swans" is an omen of the beginning of good things. come into being The Chinese letters "Ji Xiang" for improved luck and auspiciousness are above the dragon and swan. The outside border of the sign represents the power of the North Star to signify good fortune and double the prosperity. "Pak Tao Kiew Chae" is added to make the "Otagonal Swan Dragon Sign that Conquers Misfortunes" even more powerful. The back of the "Octagonal Swan Dragon Sign that Converts Misfortunes" is made up of links between both The 12 zodiacs borrow the strength of the zodiacs of each year they are born to assist diminish the force of misfortune. Im Yian's power in the middle position creates equilibrium and strengthens the power even more.

Those born in the Year of the Rabbit should also wear an auspicious pendant in the shape of the "Octangular Dragon and Swan Sign to ward off misfortune" around their necks or carry it with them when traveling outside the home, both near and far, so that their destiny is filled with auspicious treasures. Business and trade are flourishing and developing. All year, the family is tranquil and joyful. It generates greater and faster efficiency and effectiveness than previously.

.

Good Direction: Northwest, Southwest, and East
Bad Direction: West
Lucky Colors: Green, Light Blue, Black, Gray, and Blue.

Lucky Times: 05.00 – 06.59, 13.00 – 14.59, 19.00 – 21.59.
Bad Times: 07.00 – 08.59, 11.00 – 11.59, 17.00 – 18.59.

Good Luck For 2024